Sea Lilies

In memory of Ellen Michelsen
1913-2005

Sea Lilies

Selected Poems 1984-2003

John Barnie

seren

Seren is the book imprint of
Poetry Wales Press Ltd
57 Nolton Street, Bridgend, Wales, CF31 3AE
www.seren-books.com

ISBN 1-85411-413-1
A CIP record for this title is available from the British Library.

The publisher acknowledges the financial assistance
of the Welsh Books Council.

Printed in Hoefler Text by Cromwell Press, Trowbridge

Cover photo by Marty Snyderman (www.martysnyderman.com)
Back cover portrait of the author by Angharad James

Contents

Clay (1989)

from *The Confirmation* (1992)

from *At the Salt Hotel* (2003)

from *Borderland*

ENCOUNTER

Swallows flitting low
Over the grass, swimming
At our waists like
Blue-black-electric fish

Silent and buoyant, lighter
Than the air they
Breathe, gliding
Among the boles of trees.

We stand, rooted,
Or make as if to wade
Through the evening,
Heavy in our lives,

While the swallows flick
On razor wings then
Dive, air's dolphins,
Shadowing the ground.

THE STORM

I lay and heard the wind
Swear enmity to man,
How it whipped itself with wires,
Like angels cut itself in two,

To flow on, ten times ten
Strong, stronger than man. That
Was its boast. Then, in a lull,
In the underswell of its song,

I heard it cry on the wires
Like a child in a far off room,
A small cry under hearing,
And I held my breath.

NATURAL HISTORY

The dinosaurs are lucky
No longer linked by birth
And death as in two
Facing mirrors parent
To offspring. Also the dodo

Pluperfect, and the great
Auk beaten for a witch
No longer watching
Stupendous seas. And
The shark grounded in

The sands of Tennessee,
Triangular steel-blue
Components, its teeth,
Clattering in a dish
Beside artefacts and antique guns.

ETRUSCAN

Interfectus est: the perfect ending.
Power like an irritation in the bone
Drove the general on, a speartip stilled him.

Now he goes begging the other side
Of forgetting, in a toga, with a bowl
Empty of its offerings of meat, bread and wine.

Jowled, the neckskin slack, in lizard-
Folds from living well, he's more banker
Than lord. Hard for him to live in Hell,

To lie supine, while in effigy, in tufa,
He reclines on an elbow, bowl held off-
Handedly, arrogantly, on a paunchful of stone.

DECEMBER

Indisputable, impenetrable
Fog. Sometimes it wells up
Out of the river's cauldron,
Or comes down swiftly from the hills,

An old style raider.
Soon the town is lost, whirled away
On an empty planet. We keep
Our bearings: that way hills,

Down that road towns,
Staring into the white
As the day tumbles into darkness.
On a lucky night

Fog dissolves, and the hills,
Sharp as razors,
Deep as mines, grow tall,
Spangled with the beacon lamps

Of farms. Then the moon is crisp,
A high messenger of light,
And an owl's screech tethers
The woods about the town.

PATIENT GRISELDA

There's a wealth in seabirds
Pouring behind the plough,
And white sheets spread out to dry
On bushes of privet.

Radiance is from the heart,
The eye's beams turning back
To the beholder, so what she sees
She is. Scrubbing flagstones

Is a means to purity,
The foot-worn stones effaced,
Hard and yielding. My husband
Has a savage eye, asks questions,

Lives in shadows. To him
The owl's hoot is the mind's cry;
The children kicking leaves
Are suspect. He must

Knead and knead the living dough,
But cannot eat the bread. He says
I should live like him in shadow,
And hates me for the light.

THE EUROPEAN CONSCIOUSNESS

The gesture is handed down
Through history; grained film
Saying life must be like this,
Tragedy subsumed into the humdrum
Execution of the masses; piano wire
Tuned to the symphony of hanging
Faces, faces, faces. The step-
Ladder's knocked from under us,
And leaves us swinging
With the summer dead, the winter dead,
Snow crumpling under boots,
Water birds scattering from the banks,
Where the leaders, martyrs, tortured,
Peer into the flowing stream.

from *Lightning Country*

LIGHTNING COUNTRY

The larks have come down into stillness, and a wind
Whirligigs across the fields, the thick feathery wheat
In sudden buffets. Clouds the colour of plums
Cluster and ripen under the sky's dark branches.
The air could split, and the houses hold on
To their roofs; they know what's happening,
Crouched by the roads, out on the far horizon.
Rain gouts burst on darkening tarmac,
And at the world's end thunder barrels and rolls
Through an empty room, then grumbles into nothing.
The air grows chill, touchy. A zipflash
Of lightning ladders the sky; and a couple
Who were dawdling in the make-believe fields
Break into a run, rain hissing through the keeling wheat –
           magnetic north
      To the lightning's needle,
      Its quivering, steady
      Black, as the wild earth
      Flattens, ears back, like a hare.

HOME TOWN

I think of the widows; closed flowers.
Who will find them lovely, remembering
Life in the withered petals of their lips.
In morning coffee rooms
They crowd like memories, sunnily.
The make-up and the perms suggest
Summer frocks and jaunts before the war.
Now they tread to church and pray
For company. They are delicate, like moths
Found clinging to the panes on autumn
Nights. Their powdered cheeks are soft
As downy wings. Their eyes glitter
Like gems in faded boxes, blue, green,
And on fire, as many years ago.

A LETTER FROM HOME

Things are not so good here. Yesterday
I thought I heard a cry, and there he was,
Fallen over, with a wild half-comic
Stare of horror and his few black strands of hair
Awry. We got him up, and I was surprised

How soft and malleable his body
Was, and how heavy, with the stubborn weight
Of earth. He made a face of thanks
And weariness, but as if this were a message
From a long way off, and the star already dead.

IN TOUCH

Is there joy in the storm?
What you impart to it.
The night a cellophane black,
Lights snapped out,

The air a turbulence
Dark overhead. The double-gate
Kicks, a live thing,
Bucks and strikes again

Against my hands. The greenhouse –
Panes smashed – sways
Its wooden frame, straining
For release; buckles to its knees,

A felled beast. This is
The storm. All senses fleshed,
Alive, for the flying slate
Crumpling in the street,

Thudding into the lawn.
The seconds stream electrons,
Sparks of possibility,
The immensity ablaze.

THREE SCENES FROM TROY

I

When Sarpedon
Returned
Troy's pink battlements

Flashed
In the sun
Whose fiery image

Spanned the world.
What did he
Think of

On the brown paths
Home?
The fields were

Blue with cornflowers,
Wild
With tares.

II

Criseyde
Dressed in black
Whose hair was gold

Who wept
For the small birds
Limed in bushes:

Goldfinches, linnets,
With their
Fluttering wings

That dangled
By a single
Claw.

III

Behind the city
From a low, wooded hill

I heard the hunt halloo,
And turning to my window

Saw the grey hound leap
And the flashing blades of spears.

The hunting of the hart,
A bitter sport

In Troy.

THE SHEEP SAY NOTHING

Rain is the hills' weather;
Then they loom through the cloud, grey
Marie Celestes,
Laden with silence,
The captain
Gone,
The crew
Lost, stumbled off into the nothing, the hiss
And froth
Of the heather, the green
Bowing waves
Of the fern.

THE DEATH OF KING ARTHUR

When Arthur speared his nephew bastard son
Two feet through the guts, and Mordred *threste hymselff*
With alle the myght he had, up to the guard
On the old King's lance, then struck him to the brain,

A redshank probed the margins of the lake, dipping
Its head and breast, as if they hinged on its long red legs,
Sounding for molluscs in the stagnant mud. And when
The sun went down, and *robbers and pyllours* worked among the dead,

The sky was shot with stars, blazing and trailing
Through deepening space. So the large-eyed night creatures
Sniffed round the harness, the useless fingers and eyes,
Scuttling at dawn down holes, into the dark, red earth.

IN THE BLACK MOUNTAINS

We hardly know
The consequence
Of hills. Here
On this hogback

I found an owl's
White skull, and
The delicate
Piping of bones.

It was a hill
Death, clean
Like the ruined farms
Tenanted

By grass and nettles,
And silent swathes
Of light. I stood
There a long time

The only upright
Living thing, until
A wind brought cloud
Racing its

Shadow, rushing
Up hill-slopes to
Block out the sun.
What was begun

Then is with me
Now. The hills are
Impartial, out-
Lasting the farms

And the bone eyed
Owl. An open hand
Where the truth
Lies green and still.

BLACK MOUNTAINS, CODA

What are the hills like? A raven
In a thorn tree
Its one
Black fruit

That hangs
Doggedly
On

WINTER ON AGERSØ

Over the mudflats where the dunlin run
Feet in a flurry, pausing and dibbing
With nimble beaks, the sun hangs low, glittering
Its pewter light across the panels of the sea,
The watery surface of the shore. All sounds

Are bleak-edged, the waves' hissing at the small
Birds' feet, the wind rustling the stubborn tufts
Of grass. So life is almost discontinued,
Blood moving deeply and slowly through the heart,
All warmth battened down, guarded at the core.

What is there to make us adventurous, attempt
Another spring? Being burns in the sinews
And in the bones; – to be is enough, feeling the wind's
Bite on the skin, or listening to its boom and yelp
As we sit by the fire, withdrawn, with idle hands.

A FLIGHT OF STAIRS

Like a mountain climber on the highest
Reaches of a peak, stumbling in the snow,
Snatching at oxygen, you climbed each step
Of the stair. What were you expecting;
There was no way down. Gasping and crying
"Oh dear", slumped in your pyjamas to rest,
While you hauled each breath on a thin rope
From a world far below. There was greenery
There, birds and flowers; but your garden
Ran riot, your greenhouse plants were tinder.
You held up your hands to be carried on;
This was your greatest journey; you were
Beyond us, though we gripped your thin, trembling
Arms, and guided your feet where they had to go.

DELTA HARVEST

Mississippi

The houses
Squat low, they never meant
   To be here; and the trees have walked
Off
   To the skyline, they
Couldn't care; nor the vulture
   Straddling an old hair coat, bones
In the pocket.

      And the pig
Squeals once,
   But says it can take it; and the goat
Lies patiently, four feet together.
      It's all one to me,
   Says the farmer, scraping at the earth's
Skull, in a red machine,
   Under a blaze of sky.

LIME TREE

It hummed like a powerhouse,
I couldn't see why, and then,
Bees floating and hovering
Among green cumuli

That were piled high with flowers,
Where they shuttled
Attracted or repelled
By a powerful magnet.

If I touched that trunk
I might flash with a shout
Into cinder. Bees were components
In the tree's turbine,

Power building up
Through the evening, but earthed,
Unlikely to explode.
I stood drenched in scent.

Bees shipped nectar,
Stuffed pouches, bags,
Drifted in an electric hum,
Neutral to the charge.

Piratical, dark winged,
Swifts eddied, risked shock,
As bolts of black energy
Were flung from the tree.

THE CASTLE MEADOWS

Late September and the grass is drenched in cold
Dew; last martins skip and twitter over the water.
The sky is stretched and seamless, and hills about the town
Are great cathedral bells sombre with shadow. It's
Early morning. Soon the earth will be beaten down,
Last sparks of flowers and leaf stamped out
In the hedgerows, as the soil congeals, and frost
Crisps the brambles and grass, white oxide on the living
Metal. Berries will glow like dying suns, and birds flock
Like a shower of seeds flung to waste over the ploughland's
Ribs. But now in these late days, I quarter
The fields, searching the grass for the cautious
Domes of mushrooms, the tender white
That snaps off clean when I close its coolness in my palms.

THE BATTLE OF VICKSBURG

The sun sinks in its own soldering glow
And the night is nicked with needle-points of light.
Far below me, bayous deep among trees
Polish their surfaces to a last gray shine.
I stand on a rampart, a grassed-over earthwork,
Where cannon guarded the buckling bend
Into Vicksburg. The dead are everywhere,
Confederate graves and Union monuments;
And silence from the watery river lights
And winter trees. The close-cut grass
Swings up in waves over the ramparts, tosses, choppy,
On the graves. From here I could see clean into Texas,
Not a ridge or ruck in the earth
To prevent me. But darkness smudges out the land,
Turning the trees to charcoal, the river to an oily gloom.
They must have seen this by the blackening cannon
                    years before:
                    The intricate net of veins
                    And nerves, the hot core,
                    Not even a stain
                    In the soil's craw.

MOTHS

Their red eyes glow,
The ends of burning wires. Sucked
To the pane, the darkness leaves them there:
Six legs, antennae,
The wings in folds, waiting to be freed
By flapping trapped
Round a bowl of glassy light.

Yet released in daytime
They flounder for the nearest wall,
Clamped like magnets to the granuled stone.
The sun is too great
For their feathery nerves, the ruby
Madness of their eyes,
Where the unending darkness wells.

THE SECRET LIFE OF A
HOUSE AGENT'S CLERK

When she raised the blinds
I was surprised;
The grey roofs of houses, wet
With the dawn rain;

And a blackbird
Ticking its tail, in an otherwise
Empty tree. She said
I had to go.

Nothing moved in that outside world;
Not a flicker
From the closed curtains,
Eyelids at a wake.

I dressed,
And walked down the stairs, paused
In the kitchen; listened
To the clock;

Let myself out,
Released, relieved,
Into the hunger,
The street.

MORTE DARTHUR

After the cries had echoed from the hollows
Darkness fell. It was autumn, and an early frost
Had crusted on the armour like an old man's stubble,
Crystals bristling as they grew under the fierce
Unsteady stars. The moon came out like a widow
Bending over the field, but there was none she knew
Young or old, locked in the armour
Of stiffening sinews. She went her way keening
Across the sky. The only sounds these knights could muster
Were a champing horse's shaken bridle
And gasses bubbling from the slain. "I think," said Malory,
"The stars are flying from us, and the light we see
May come from suns already dead." Turning
The pages of the book, with its vivid pictures
Of the times. So he died, and nurses touched his eyes,
Prizing the book from puffy hands,
                    one finger
            Sliding from the place
            Where dawn comes up
            And crows alight in flocks
            On frosted shrouds.

NOVEMBER STORM

Wind heading east today
With a job to do; trees
To uproot, and slates to flip
Like crazy coins from the roofs.

There's a roaring in the air
Miles deep, and the birds are gone,
Except the ground-level sparrows
Slap-dashed into shelter.

This is the time I like,
The light sharp steel in a moil
Of clouds, any second to snap
And spin into the ground. The city

Hunkers in mud,
Crude as a kraal,
And all our expensive lives
Lie down with fear.

BOTANICAL GARDENS

Seeds drift in peaceable flocks, white feathery tufts
That lodge in the hair. Here is an alpine outcrop
With glittering rocks and thin soil, where rockplants
Crawl beneath the breeze and harebells tintinnabulate
On one-strand, quivering wire stems. Down by the lake
A snake slips like greased steel through marsh plants,
The thick mash of green; and in the hot-house,
Palmtrees and ferns press giant fronds to the glass
Like moonish prisoners peering out at life.
Everything's controlled; there's a list of rules
And the gardens close at six. It's a fangless world
Where blue tits flicker to the hand for food
And mallards doze with zipped-up eyes, their necks
Polished by the sun to a regimental shine.
                    Outside,
              The city squats like a toad
              With unblinking eyes;
              Mottled and blotched and poisonous;
              Hoarding this ornament in its head.

HOW TO WATCH BIRDS

Shallows of the sea frozen over in sheets,
Crackling panes of ice that split, squeaked under foot,
And in between, wrinkled sand like buried ribs.
The tide was turning, sneaking in under the ice,
Cold runs of water like the clearest crystal.
We walked on the sand, wavered, slid, on the creaking sea,
And a steely wind tortured tears from our eyes,
So the world wobbled, flashed ripple-light
Off water and ice, while the cold dug deep
Into our bones, and the wind hammered our skulls.
Doug had brought brandy which we drained in large gulps,
And the glow-coloured liquid left us no warmer.
We were defeated. But the great black-backed gulls,
Redshanks and shelducks and barrel-chested geese
Stayed on, foursquare on ice or seafrozen stones,
Staring into the wind. We lurched, lunged back
                    to the road.
              My head banged with pain
              The cap of bone too cold
              To touch, the wrinkled brain
              Hunched in its hole, like a toad.

Clay

TABLE TALK

I

On the banks of the Susquehanna
The servant lies down with the master
Though in the mind. Coleridge married Sara
And was unhappy ever after. – Byron
Had a pantisocracy of his own;
He fluttered like doves the petticoats
Of the serving girls of the Abbey. –
On this grey day walking by the river
Who do you wish was with us? The water
Ruffled in shallows, glittering the same
Freak pattern over stone. A fish jumps – see –
But you never see the leaping form
Caught at its apogee; the monumental,
Momentary, contentment in the sun.

II

Byron set the dog to guard against
Visiting Cockney poets whose children
Scribbled on the walls of his hired
Italian palazzo. Principles of Education!
Damnation in the billiard room;
The bull dog flopped on the cool marble
With glum salivating jaws. Mrs H.
Unravelled grievance as she did her knitting.
Italy was hot; the children awful.
Milordo Inglese tempered satire
With desire for pain. Verse was a joke
Scribbled after dining. That summer
Letters crossed the grand, heroic Alps,
Complaining of domesticity, and loss.

III

Coleridge hard at work at being busy –
"Did you ever hear me preach, Charles?"
"The Watchman" followed by "The Friend".
Men like Wordsworth left him no time
Perched forever on a ledge of the mind.
"Of Coleridge I shall say nothing –
Why he may divine." Left scampering
From the window to the door, on a day,
The garden sopping, blackbirds in their graves.
Books, books, books; German philosophy
Itching in the mind. Sara, and Sara,
That consequential name. Spare half a thought,
Release me from trampling in the mire.
Life the disease, my death the only cure.

FLOOD

Shelley

Autumn came in hesitant starts,
Wind cracking our skin out of the north,
Then days when the earth was still with astonishment
That anything could, in its being,
Be so beautiful. Peasants warned us
Of October rains. One night of thunder
And lightning the streams choked, stormed
Onto the plain. Now living-rooms
Are sullen with vomit tide-marking the walls;
The brown sheet of water moves among houses
Unresisted, or swirls and frowns,
Ruffled on a snag. Far out, a bonfire
Guides peasants, horses, cows over a ford:
It's high ground tonight with a shrug of the shoulders.
The red light of its flame shivers in oils
Across the flood, dark shapes of animals and men
Stumbling past its glare then gone.
I can't hear their shouts or the bullocks' moans.
Waggons are abandoned, the brown force
Would shoulder them away, cant them,
Whirl them like Dervishes drowning in their skirts.
It's quiet now, somewhere the river
Dreams of its banks in a deep sleep.
Mary sleeps with the child.
                              When lightning
Cracked round our house with a bluish hue
Sulphurous and deadly, it shocked our faces
By its eagle-glare. I'll write poems, dark glass,
Through which you'll look at unkillable light.

CLAY

Coleridge

"Promise." I was a fine sight, setting out.
I could annotate a book in minutes,
Fillet the thought from the words' integument.
It was a party trick – friends clapped,
Lent me their books to be marginally glossed.
I could quote "auctoritee" till midnight.
Last night the moon lay hidden by a cloud,
A dark, uncomprehending mass; but light
Brightened its edges, streamed into the sky
Softening the gloom. I waited minutes,
Minutes... the cloud was a sullen beast,
The one I have felt upon my back
Deadening my joy, turning me to clay.
I stood then as if looking at myself.

We're all wandering, though some don't know it.
William looks at me down his long thin nose:
"Not I my friend." We haven't met in years...
I remember his disapproving glance.
Why am I the failure? His verse goes on
Like well-intentioned knitting. My life
Revolved round plans, I was the architect,
Blueprints of the mind scattered about.
Friends looked in to admire the proposition:
"This will be great." Everything was mind,
Platonic, a vast uncharted land.
I grappled with immense ideas. Applause!
Prometheus must come to earth with fire.
Who set store by an empty-handed hero?

FROM MY JOURNAL
Byron

Parma ham has a dried blood look,
The fat a smokey cream. Italians
Praise God they aren't English, so do I.
That weakling Keats dying at twenty-five,
Though the man was a poet "for a' that".
Scotch blood and Italian women
Mix well. The Hunts have arrived – a Gypsy camp.
What should they think? Leigh with a laugh
And a toss of the head, the wife a frump
At thirty. They drift from room to room,
Exchange glances in mirrors. Tomorrow
I'll take him shooting: a silver Thaler
Set in a stick and swung like a pendulum.
Famous poet! The Hunts look grumpy. Not I.

• • •

"Death's a cheat. The 'Great Leveller'
Smooths out distinction, but difference
Makes us human. At the Last Trump
Who'd 'warble hymns' in Heaven with a chance
To plot in Hell? Satan's an angel
Glimmering in the dark, who refused for us
God's crust. After I'm dead the Grand Guignol
In sulphurous caves will suit me well."

A hush. Mario pours more wine.
Intelligence is a fine thing. Bait
The middle class and let it pass for play.
Candles glisten in the Hunts' eyes.
Each night as they lie in bed – I can tell –
They hold hands and wonder why they came.

1798

Hazlitt

Who is this man in a sky blue coat,
A preacher with ideas on everything?
I walked with him ten miles from Wem,
Stepped on his heels as he skipped and veered
Trammelled by the confines of the road.
Yesterday, from a coach, a field of poppies
Stiff as pokers, stripped of their flowers,
Flowed by, seed-pods ripe to be milked
Or stewed into a soothing liquor.
I thought of that day and our setting out,
Nothing could be so promising or pure.
We stopped at an inn before parting.
A bad brew makes a bitter drink.
We supped too long and never could be friends.

Coleridge

I remember only his father
Sitting in a corner, faintly disapproving.
I could talk on twenty subjects then
Aphorisms, truth, truisms and twaddle.
We each botched a marriage, I to endure,
He to escape to a back kitchen slut
Via a Scotch divorce. *Liber Amoris!*
Who hasn't had enough of love?
Cut-and-run, or bind the knot tighter,
He ended up no happier than me.
They say I've been a disappointment –
So none should doubt, when I reach the pass,
I'll kiss my wandering friends goodbye.
I once was a preacher who preached to stones.

MARY SHELLEY

Like a sycamore's winged seed, brought down –
"Are you that damned atheist Shelley?"
Three children buried should have been enough.
Post-haste – the wheels of his carriage
Clatter across Italy. In the maremma the frogs –
Grex-grex, grex-grex. He told the men of England
In no uncertain terms... In his glass tower
He could see the wind build storms.
Peace, miserable peace; his name was a byword;
Whenever was there peace for me.
Show me your scars, mine stretch across my belly.
The doors are open for a wind to blow in,
Cooling my face and ruffling the curtains.
We never closed them anywhere we lived...
Books, bundled into coaches, boxes,
Left scattered, called for, lost; like letters
Never arriving and perhaps not sent.
Father was a better dun than the courts,
Shelley's banknotes, gold and drafts kept him,
A door onto a ruin, implacable.
Someone lived there once. My mother?
Byron eats biscuits to keep the body thin,
But the souls of these poets are fat, fat.
Shelley comes and asks, "Shall we dress for dinner?
I'm tired of this déshabillé."
The noble lords of England. Throw down the whip,
There's still the spur. And the frogs go
Grex, grex-grex, grex-grex, grex... grex.

BLAKE'S DREAMS

I

I'll burn through these doors. The universe is – is –
The mind's a mantrap – most tread gingerly
Afraid it will spring. I'd hang gladly
To leap into the world within.
Life was never a prison to me.
Sapience – restraint, control – chains melt
In the mind's acetylene flare.
You, you, and you, who know nothing.
Sparks shower from the cutting edge,
Dance and bounce on the floor. – Soon to be through! –
You'll not look – but I'll look –
I'll splinter your parallelograms –
Words in your book will darken and burn –
I'll stand and be elected by the light.

II

Look at this now... acid's snakey lines;
It's the devil's work dissolving metal.
Such dilutions... careful calculations.
And all for an imprint on the page
Of my dreams. – Half of you to spurn them,
Fall into death and rot –
The natural way with mankind.
You'll have plenty of prophets –
Bible-Jacks who drink cold water
And vomit lies. Who stands for truth
Must pass the test himself – plunge in
Head and shoulders through the flames.
You see nothing... but I see a treadmill
Rattling in sunlight to a flurry of feet.

COLERIDGE TO LAMB

"Pass the butter, Mary, and poke the fire.
This evening there's a draught at every door.
Cloud wraps the moors in its dirty rag
And rain comes tapping at the pane politely
Though there's no admittance here.
I'd sooner lose a hundred lines of verse
Than tramp the moors tonight. Tea is a comfort
Steaming in the cup." And when I stirred
To speak, a firm hand pressed me back:
"Dear William is never interrupted."
"They are everything to me, my girls...
There is much to do, the garden to plant,
And a new collected *Works*." I left
The poet "at home". Charles, who'd live like that.

CONSUMED WITH FIRE

Byron

Trelawney juggled Shelley's heart
Out of the coals of his body.
The Cornishman's oven trembled in the heat
And the air drove up so violently
It seemed combustible, and that
A sheet of flame must sweep his soul
Into the sky. Not a bit of it.
The brain bubbled in the skull's kettle
And faugh! as London beaux might say,
The stench in the updraught taught
Here was a poet entirely human.
What the carabinieri thought – milordo
With a hand before his mouth,
Another smouldering in a homemade oven –

I cannot say, their uniforms
And moustachios shimmering in the heat,
An Italian fata morgana;
Dark-eyed, mournful, indifferent men.
How long it takes bones to burn down!
"Tre." worried like a cook around the stove,
Piled on more wood and peered inside:
"A heart won't burn that's gorged with blood."
So Shelley submitted to the physics
Of flesh. And that is all there is.
Trelawney gave the wife his heart.
Which one: I'll not say. All around's
Indignity, dishonour, loss.
Operatic? This endgame was pure farce.

THE QUARREL
Coleridge

Slander by the fireside; a letter warning
Of "our Friend"... who might impose. I know his style.
Etceteras and innuendo,
Hesitation with a downcast eye.
Now the truth's out I'll tell you the truth,
I never liked him nor his women
Who dote like cows and skip to his command.
He was always the wind to his own sail
And none dared embark on his little sea...
I left and made the hard walk to the pass;
Rain chilled my back and I never turned.
What pettiness. The grandeur of the storm
And I could only think of him; two hearts
Calcined in the flames of mutual hate.

Wordsworth

"I think it consistent with my duty..."
(How hard it is to write the truth)
"True Friendship, as the Ancients knew..."
(This pen's too delicate, and my writing
Spidery. Mary, a penknife and a quill)
"Dear C. has been all-in-all to me,
Yet early as Alfoxden days
I saw his sliding heart..." (And knew at once
The obligation placed upon the strong)
"You will appreciate, I know, that I
Have no interest..." (This is an affair
Must break the chain binding him to me)
"I remain etcetera." (It is written.
Signed. The blow delivered by my hand).

THOMAS JEFFERSON HOGG

Paper fire-boats sped off to burn and sink...
Again and again. I stood, hands in pockets.
Fire was his medium but water claimed him.
Harriet drowned like a stage Ophelia
Big with child. Shelley's ideas... scaffolding
He climbed to see the Earth. His visions – straw –
But men tread water reaching out for less.
We were diversions from the airy building.
Now he's dead I sit with his poems
Heavy on my lap of an evening.
His fire was cold, not Promethean –
A coloured flame of the wicked magician
For the children's little show. After,
Cups and blancmanges to clear away,
Guests packed in coats, goodbyes at the door.
What then? His mind bent in light
Like a stick thrust in sunlit water.
A November wind rustles up leaves
And slaps them blackening across the earth.
He burned with a flame "that refines not
Nor consumes". I was afraid
To touch those intellectual hands.
Fire danced in the rigging of his mind,
Its flames bred their opposite in me.
I'll cling with the leaves... and at the last
Be rattled quickly through the streets,
Content, like the rest, in an ordinary way
To be wrapped, forgotten, in the earth.

A NIGHTMARE

Crabbe

Fresh water trapped in the couplet's granite,
Held under pressure. Grimes in his boat
Maundering among reeds, water flat and filmy
With oil of decay. The good preacher
Bends to his quill; whole villages must be
Penned in, ironed and starched in rhyme.
We must breathe – strait-laced is strangle-held.
Polished boots of iamb stride across the page,
Characters cry out, elbowing, angry,
Fall to the scythe of rhyme and moulder
In suitable graves. Tombstones lean
Confidential and foolish. Gat-toothed the living,
Arm-wrestled by the preacher into verse.

BYRON AT MISSOLONGHI

God's a conservative, like me,
And knows freedom only leads to choice,
The wrong one naturally, and death,
But gave it us in the Earth's first garden.
Perfection's an alabaster statue,
Harmless marble, nudity and drapes
In a hundred noble galleries.
God likes art, the something out of reach,
Marred, the artist daring to stop short,
Or wringing his hands on publication day
(More likely) at the world's reserved applause.
For we prefer completion, faultlessness,
The heavenly divine collaboration
Of the rules and schools. I've no such patience,
All my poems are leaky tubs, and Juan the best
Like a shipwright's nightmare. So I'm here,
Helping the Greeks help their shady selves
As God intended, the mote that makes creation
Art. I'll drink to that, one artist to another.
History books will shirk the issue:
Hero of the Greeks, who fought off fat
No better than the Turks. But dying
In a marshland town, who cares. Frogs croak-croak
Or plop in pools at an approaching shadow;
Like the masses they'd rather not know fear
But live out their lives on lily pads.
Greeks think revolution is for this:
Kill the Turks, the sun will shine forever.

WORDSWORTH

Parsimony, always a family trait,
Though a dole of love may be a parsec
To the stars: small measurement
For inconceivable space. Ask my Mary
Though not my friends, whose tongues
Have been a kourbash to my name.
Envy's a sour nut to crack in middle age,
It furs the mouth, and the righteous
Wash it down with rich, red, angry port.
I did only my best for them:
Sometimes the goad, sometimes a polished apple.
We all die in loneliness of heart,
I've seen many grow quiet, though
To the outward eye they seemed familiar,
The husk mistaken for the grain;
But the blaze that impelled them
Had shrunk to a small hearth fire. In the end
They gave up any thought of warmth
And the animating soul slipped away.
It's hard to let go: we clutch their hands
For their resolve questions ours...
But at last they're still; the hands' leaves
Shrivelled and dry that drummed
With ideas; lifted pale-side, dark-side,
As a wind struggled in branches
Shattering sunlight onto the grass.
In age, it's too late to call a new tune,
The piper and his penny-whistle gone.

PALIMPSEST

Wordsworth puts down his book
And just steps out, he won't be long.
Coleridge at the apothecary
Knows there is a cure for a branching
Restlessness of mind; he must still the stars
Dancing above the wind-tossed wood.
Byron strikes a pose, pours from his fist
A whispering pyramid of salt
On the cloth before the Hunts. Dinner is over,
"So much for life." So much shining
From what they left, the half-life of their lives
A powerful radiation.

Summer's honouring its pact with winter,
The Earth in disarray, profusion,
A vast scattering of seeds, nuts, fruits,
Beyond the need of squirrels, drunken wasps
Or men. Beech mast, acorns, crunch underfoot,
The month of October is heroic,
Lavish before the end.
                          They were the same,
The same impetus powering a green season
Driving their poems to blossom and fruit
Beyond any need. For fuel
They fed it their lives, gave
What was needed to ruthlessness of art,
Conferred suffering on others
As well as themselves, roots that go deep
In the wet black mould of earth.

from *The Confirmation*

LEAVING

The new life!
It seems like every turn
Opens a vista: those hills!
That estuary! People –

At the end of the journey
Suitcase unpacked,
There's the same old face
To be shaved,

Barefaced, there's the same
Old lie. It's hard
To change. The good thief
Was too good; the bad

Like most, hoped
Against the chance
That at sundown events
Would set him free.

"I never knew."
"I never thought."
The leopard washed in soap's
As good as new,

As old. He looks around.
Cut from the cross,
Wounds healed, the thief
Turns corners, steals again.

GRASS

Even a lawn
As it whimpers underfoot
Inches sideways –

Not like a sycophant
But one with a grasp on things. Cut back,
Chopped out,

Grass plays small
In the shadow of man.

Left a year, lawns riot to
Tussocks,
Uncombable shambles.

We prefer clipped dress,
But a lawn's déshabillé
Is right

For the rough lout, steaming in November sun,
Dumb and sullen
Under frost.

Grass waits.
Even the keenest mower dies,
And over his grave

Humped like a mummy-case
Or flat like a door
It will grow

The mower's last green coat.

WINTER NIGHT: WALKING ON THE SEA

Stand on the sea's crust,
Surface churned and salted
But level-steady. How thick?
The foot prods cautiously,
Tests for weight. It holds.
A foot and a foot,
You're further out. Get back!
Someone on shore dances,
Gesticulates. Too late,
You're here, it dares you,
Foot and a foot on ice
Fragile as iron.
The crust creaks, plates
Compacted together. One
Could tip like a lid
On a black hole of water,
You'd slide like a corpse
In the sea. "Come back!"
Somebody calling you.
Gauge ahead... rigid ice
In a pact – "I'll bear you" –
Beneath, the shelving, sly
Black sand, blind water
With its eyes tight shut.
Whiteness cherishes you
On this dark night; glimmers
In hope. Walk for miles,
The last lone figure. "Come back!"
Turn again to the dark line of trees,
Party-lights in a house.
Retrace, retread a path
On the ice, whispering trap,
Gritting its teeth.

PARALLEL LINES

What a surprise:
The white surface
Of the moon, a face
In shock, hair torn off,

On what I thought
Was an ordinary
Day, floating in blue.
And here come gulls

In a keen cruise,
Intent on their doings
Like the motion
Of silence.

Blood and bone
Keep me trudging
While the gulls spill air
To harbour in a field

And the moon
Fades as if the future
Were a self-effacement
Into the past.

LATER

When I'm too old for scrambling
Up and down the hills
And valleys of sex, I'll
Rethink my position,

Look at water
Under a microscope,
The study of clarity;
Float pollen in its lens

Till the nuggets and shields
Come clean
As Trojan gold. I'll enjoy
The facelessness

Of that; the worth
Of nothing. Then
I might take silence
In sunlight,

Listening for its hiss
In interstices
Of leaves. I'll sit
With the surface

Of a white page,
And think of cleanness
In a mind prepared to leave.
Everyone else

Will carry on
Living with the red shift,
Each believing of the other:
"He is saying goodbye."

FIRST STEPS IN ASTRONOMY

Stars crackle their rockets
In the glossiest black
Deeper than measurable
Distance. But the eye

Is drawn to the moon,
How it changes from gold
To white at dawn
Like news of a death,

Yet is buoyant, dissolves,
In face of the sun's
Bleak furnace;
As if matter were

Immaterial, to be
Seen through, the mind
Disengaged from its pacing
Up and down. Though I like

Sharp life, the blackbird's
Brilliant stare,
A trowel's edge
Swept through cement,

It is good to know
How matter floats
In dandelion clocks through space
Light as a breath.

OUT OF THE FIGHT

The black graves of the Cymry
On impossible slopes,
Giving back no light but
Absorbing all into the stone,

The colour of umbrellas
And sombre clothes and hushed
Conversation; future plans
Brought to an end

With the chisel's clean
Strokes. At dawn, even,
The lanes and roads are filled
By the whine of traffic,

A great army revving up,
Full of expectation,
About to launch an offensive
In all directions.

The absence of sound
About the stones cannot be
Broken; absolute zero
Of such active expectations.

A WORM

Squirts itself from earth in a jet-pipe of panic

A long-pink muscle pumping itself

Flowing to the end of the tip's rubber rattle

One-arm wrestling in the grass

Released by a trowel jarred on stone

A glissando trawled alive from the soil

Somebody's hair-bow that's about to scream

Fat ribbon wriggling off the old man's parcel

A death dive into light

The delirious patient who flops on the floor

A churning red knot of anger

The rope of pork slithering at the table edge

And it's gone – down among roots

A last flick of the tail's attenuated nipple

The girl with anorexia laid at last to rest

PHANTOMS

Unstable as herds,
Ears pricked, heads turned
From their feeding. Men
Duck under wings
With fuel pipes; trucks

Sidle up with missiles.
The canopies bulge
As the eye that sees fear
In all directions.
It will stampede them,

Gazelles on the runway
Shimmering in giddy heat,
Lifting and folding their
Legs in an act of grace
As they leap with our lives.

EYES CLOSED

Eyes closed because he had no more use for them
Too busy with the inner life and a thought
Told him by a voice that whispered important things
Until he stopped his breath and strained his inner ear
Listening to what he had waited for, for a lifetime.
When the body remembered, it snatched at a breath,
Then the deep listening over again. At last the body forgot,
Stillness passed between us, and I had to cry for the loss;
Not his, but mine. I wanted to know what was said
That calmed him after so much suffering.

AIEE!

Ah the old, leaving
Forget-me-nots
At the grave. My mother
Now telling the story

Again. Patience sits
Hands over ears
And conscience wrings
Dry tears from a cloth.

NO

I don't want those gristly
Hands slipping toward
Me over the counterpane

Patched purple under
The cuticle with blood
From the slightest knock

Offering a blessing
And aching to receive
As much as they give.

VEXED

The elder sits
Like one round whom the rest
Must warm themselves.
But the tales won't kindle
Any more. She tells again
What a glow there used
To be. The children are bored,
And the man
Beats his hands against
An anger,

The battleship
In an alien river
Of a people he must
Not blast away.

ROOF FALL

Backful of brittle bones,
Ankles swollen,
Finger-joints a display case
For arthritis, yet

The head can still swivel
And the brain yawn
Its old stories out.
Ma, the mamau, heartless

As caves where they once
Died as beasts
In their yearning for
Love. Hunt them out.

MOTHER

A dandelion clock
Half blown away, the face
Tilted up for a kiss.
"Have you missed me?"
Teeth inside the cheeks'
Wrinkled pouches
Mull things over.
"Having come this far,
Am I to be the witness
Of my own defeat?"

I CAN'T KEEP THEM BOTH

– "I can't keep them both, Ma. There's no money and he's always
                                                        drunk."
At the bottom of the long cottage garden was a buttercup field.
In summer it was glazed with foot-high flowers.
– "Let's see if you like butter."
And Grandma leaned over the low wall to pick a spray,
Holding it to my chin.– "You do."
When the pig had to be killed, she fed it special scraps,
Rubbing its back with a broom.
But when the butcher came, with men to hold it down, she was stern.
I knelt by the bucket with a wooden spoon.
– "Stir it thoroughly."
The slash across the throat was quick and well-done,
And as it bucked and screamed, blood pumped into the bucket.
Then the pig relaxed, as if it had taken it kindly.
The men let go and it flopped to one side.
– "There you are, Mrs Fletcher." – "Thank you, Mr Jones."
I walked to the end of the garden and stood at the wall.
Buttercups moved a shimmering cloth in the breeze.
– "Melva! Melva! Mecky!"
That year Grandma had held me up to a hedge where thrushes
    crammed a nest with their beaks;
But boys next door had stuffed them to the jaws with sand and they
    died.
Mother had been urgent in that talk in the kitchen.
The coconut matting had prickled my knees, linoleum cool on my
    palms,
As I listened, pressed close to the dark side of the door.

I SWISHED A HAND THROUGH LANE GRASS ON MY WAY TO SCHOOL

I swished a hand through lane grass on my way to school.
Under the clock Mr Rosser waited till the late boys came.
– "Hold out your hand."
Standing back he slashed six weals across palms, pacing the strokes.
Each returned to his seat holding a hand at its wrist
As if it belonged to another and must be carried carefully.
I was six and winced.
Yet one of the boys told me later he was glad.
He'd joined the Navy when war broke out;
Onboard, recruits had to climb the mast,
And if they failed had to try again, jeered from below.
This one climbed beyond the rigging,
Shinning so far up the varnished wood the deck became silent.
A gull sheered past.
He clung to the mast that shivered under him.
To the east were docks and the extended smudge of a city;
To the west, flint-coloured water that lightened in patches from
    cuffs of the wind.
He looked about him, then down.
Upturned faces stood in the pools of their shadow,
The third mate apart, not daring to command.
– "Outclimb pettiness and you're free; that's the danger of discipline
    and fear."
He clambered back, step by step, out of the air.
When his feet touched the deck, he turned at their level,
But the officer never looked him in the face.

MY COUSIN TOLD ME THIS

My cousin told me this.
Just after the war when everything was grey and empty
He worked on a coaster sailing for Emden,
The kind that takes anything and asks no questions.
But this was a government job, ballast going out
And a return over the greasy winter swell with German bombs.
The sea was so cold herring gulls rode rough salt-pats of ice that
    littered the water,
Wings furled, bodies held steadily under the shifting balance of their
    feet.
The third trip, my cousin says, was the same as the others,
Ballast out then back over the cold water with bombs,
Until as they neared the English coast the engines stopped
And the engineer told the captain he'd told him so
Then clanked his boots back down into the depths.
The thrum of engines is like the ticking of a clock, only noticed when
    it stops.
With nothing to do, my cousin leaned over the rail
And listened to the quiet slap of water against rusted iron.
A mile off were cliffs and a brightly lit building.
Nothing happened until a following wind blew up and on a turning
    tide
The ship began to drift, dragging its anchors.
The captain swore at the engineer and the engineer read the captain
    something he'd prepared for a long time in his mind.
But the ship was driven steadily toward the cliffs
Until now it could be seen that the lights were a ballroom
With a large revolving mirror-glass globe
Shooting its bits of glitter out across the walls and dancers.
The men's dark suits and the women's peach and lime, mauve and
    blue ball-gowns
Drifted in a rhythmic haze of foxtrots, waltzes and quicksteps,
Then everyone drew back as a couple stamped out a Latin-American
    number
To a lot of applause. But of course all this took place in silence seen
    from the drifting ship.

You had to imagine the middle-ageing ten-piece band that had played
    before the war,
The brylcreemed leader turning spryly to the audience,
Conducting the band unnecessarily from behind.
And you had to imagine the saxophones' riffs
And mutes on the trumpets wa-waaing through another Forties' hit.
While he was watching all this, luckily at some point, my cousin says,
The anchors held and the ship strained in the swell beneath the cliffs
And the flashing lights of the ballroom where dancers whirled and
    laughed and had never known
Such a time. Well it was after the war, but, my cousin says,
What we think of as the bright surface of things
Must be held close to its partner, an immutable truth,
The darkness within and beneath that sometimes moves to kill you
    with intent,
And sometimes drifts just short of blowing up the show.

RATS

The bakery had a high ceiling and windows with many panes.
It should have been light and airy, but only the top panes opened
By pulling on long waxed cords that hung in slack loops.
The whitewashed walls and painted pipes were grey in any light
And the air thin, dry with flour-dust
Floating in sunbeams or swirled up as a baker passed by.
We breathed it in as it settled on the pipes
Where rats ran with their crouched intentions.
We snatched lumps of dough, threw them as they scuttled past at
    shoulder height
But always missed,
Leaving the walls spattered with mementos.

In the evening we left the dough to itself in large bins,
Until at dawn it had risen to a swollen, clammy skin,
Ticking and spitting as it stretched.
After we had weighed out the loaves and let them prove,
We pushed them deep into the stifling ovens.
The foreman sang mock-tenor, inflated by the room
– "O so-le MI-O"
Then la-lahed rashly through the tune.
Rats pattered over the pipes; halted to sniff; hung their tails down
    like an untied lace.

– "Look at that one, Johnny!"
The singer stopped to point. When the river had flooded and sewers
    backed up into the town,
He'd found a large rat, drenched and shivering in the toilet,
And after it had rubbed along the wall into a corner,
He'd jabbed it to death unskilfully with a broom.
– "You'd be surprised how rats can leap."
He showed me the puncture marks on his chin: four holes neatly
    pincered together.
– "Nothing would make it unlock. I had to twist its neck with a click
As it clung to me, scrabbling in air with its feet."
Men clanked bins to the sinks, with laughter and echoing shouts.

SEEING HIM SIT

Seeing him sit in front of his greenhouse
With a two-inch belt round his trousers,
Arms akimbo and thinning hair brushed back,
I would never think he had been a desert dentist
Breaking ranks like the others when they passed a dead Turk,
Kneeling softly beside him to look into his mouth,
Then prizing out the malleable gold
With the point of a knife. Each had a pouch at his belt
Drawn together at the neck with a thong, and in went the irregular
    pieces of gold.
So the pouch got heavier as the march went on. Sometimes
They tramped through marshes with thick black pools of oil and
    bubbling gas,
And he said the irony was men poured out half a pouch of fillings
    for one tin mug
Of beautiful, colourless water. And as they put back their heads
    to drain it,
He noticed the action of their throats swallowing, as sharply as
    anything he had seen before.

I HAD CLIMBED THE LONG SLOPE

I had climbed the long slope of the spur from Capel Madog to Banc-y-
Darren
Where the hedgerows of blackthorn leaning away from the western
wind
Thin out to be replaced by stiff fence-posts of weathered wood
That are always grey, strung with rusted barbed wire, for the last few
miles.
On the field banks with their thin feathers of upland grass, harebells
raised soft blue flowers
And bushes of gorse the rough intense green of their canopies.
Nobody walked here, and a wheatear ahead of me had a moorland
tameness,
Flitting along fence-posts as I came, with its rich buff-and-grey, black
mask, black wings and tail.
On either side parallel ridges were grouped in rough lines and to the
north
Cader Idris was a grey wash rugged with bulk.
In the summer light the sea's geometric plane canted up to the horizon
where
So indistinct the eyes strained to believe them, the hills of Pen Llŷn
Were islands, a rubbing of deeper blues between sky and water.
On the highest point of the ridge I'd stopped to look back, then
turned
To the six houses of Banc-y-Darren strung at the throat
Of my ridge and the next, where I'd make my descent.
Out of the hills beyond, a speck hurtled ahead of itself,
A Phantom, nose tearing through the silk and pressure of the air.
In such a still world the eye follows anything that moves.
On across the valley parallel to where I stood,
It was beautiful as a harebell or a wheatear.
As it reached me, it was still ahead of its sound, as if its power were
silence
Fuelled by the land its shadow fled across.
I could see the tanks slung under the wings
And the two grey missiles
Slim and leaning at the end of the tightened leash.
And through the clear canopy I saw Cader Idris beyond
And that the Phantom was empty.

Then the power of the engine buckled and crumpled the air,
Sound chasing this marvel which sped ahead in perfection.
It diminished to a spot until I knew it must be over the sea,
And when my sight felt that almost it must snap
And that now I could see it and now not, the Phantom fell in the
    slowest of curves,
Its fuel tanks exhausted.
The earth around me had absorbed the shock of the engine
And now in the sea there was a short white punctuation
That rose to a silent spume, then settled back
In the canted water.
The wheatear still flicked ahead of me from fence to fence
And I walked on to Banc-y-Darren
Past the few mountain ash that every year
Try out leaves above branches and trunks
That will never be more than crippled in the poor soil of these fields.
And I passed, on either side of the lane,
Houses with names and ordinariness,
Flowerbeds and cars, the modernized cottage and the picture-window
    bungalow,
Everything as it ought to be, yet right and not right,
As if, though there would be deaths, there would also be days
People living here would call "tomorrow", with confidence.

THE TOWN WHERE I WAS BORN

The town where I was born is surrounded by hills.
When the evening sky shone turquoise in summer, with small ribs of
    cloud,
And Venus wobbling its brilliance on the horizon,
The hills became solid black without any depth.
Even a farm light gave no perspective, or the lamps of a car
Bumping up to a flash then disappearing
As it twisted down a lane between banks and trees.
And when the night was grey with cloud from the Llangattock
    Mountains
To the Black Mountains across the Usk,
The hills were muggy and insecure, withdrawn without feature,
Except over the Blorenge where the under-surface of cloud had a
    reddish tinge
From the flaring of blast-furnaces in the town beyond.
There was a steady glow, with occasional flickering, like a colour of
    silence,
And I had to strain to think of the roar and shouts
As liquid steel trundled overhead in cauldrons on chains
To be poured with a shower of sparks in moulds
By men who moved quickly in the heat and glare.
Now things are different: I am another man and look at other hills.
Last night I stood on the doorstep after dark and stared into the east
    as if it were the past.
I could guess where Craig-y-Pistyll plunged down
And where was Bryn Garw among the invisible folds,
But all was embedded in dark. I thought: it is without and within,
Watching a car on the long track from Banc-y-Darren
Travel down through Cefn Llwyd, faltering lights that rose to a glare,
As if they were looking for something.
This time the cloud glowed too, and because the wind had veered
    through the day from south to east,
I could smell them burning, Birmingham and Coventry,
And the red glowering of the sky was the reflection of their flames,
And across Pumlumon, Liverpool and Manchester, and across
    Mynydd Epynt,
Cardiff and Bristol. The cloud slid steadily above me
And on the wind there was the smell of the fine dust of bricks

And the black dust of charcoal, and the grey dust of stones.
I never knew before how the smell of cities burning
Is like the must and acridity of old houses and the lives they have
   given up.
I remembered how in Cardiff after the war, we passed rows of façades
And nothing else standing, and how in a second-floor window for a
   year
There was a wine-glass intact, missed by the blast,
Placed there by the hand which had drained it and moved away
With a shining clarity, a salute and goodbye.

AT CRAIG-Y-PISTYLL

At Craig-y-Pistyll there's a deserted house
This side of the rocky gully that takes excess water from the dam.
With the door ajar and burst from its hinges
I didn't need to knock before I went in,
And black-and-red tiles in square patterns
Led me to the living-room where grey light from a small window
Showed me tools with smooth handles no one had a use for,
And a long-shafted spade for pulling bread deftly from the oven
In a deep recess by the grate. And there were chairs, unvarnished,
And looking as though they were made to be patient in.
In the kitchen nothing but bare stone, and bottles on a shelf,
Green and brown glass with dust round the necks.
Going up the dried wood of the narrow stairs
Was still like intruding on a privacy,
Bending to peer through dirty panes in low windows,
Wandering the four rooms across echoing planks.
But there were holes in the roof where slates had slipped
And the open sky was a greater intrusion.
In the shed outside there had been sheets of hardboard,
Beams of rough-cut wood (none of it new),
The hardboard buckling slightly from being stacked
At too broad an angle against the wall.
And wandering into a final bedroom
I found a double-bed wrapped in black polythene.
Lying back, I stared through a hole in the roof
And listened to wind in nearby trees.
Whoever had been here with timber and hardboard
Had lain as well on the damp-free shining mattress and slept,
Or not slept but turned at last on his back to look at the clouds
    flushed by the moon
And clusters of stars that could have been galaxies
Shimmering faintly in the holes above his head.
Then he heard the silence as defined by leaves
And the intricate movements of a stream meandering in shallows a
    hundred yards from the house.
The bread spade, the useless tools and the stripped farmhouse chairs
    had been his,

Not the left-overs of people giving up and leaving the door open
    without looking back
Following the bitter jutting of their jaws.
Even in summer he felt chilly on the bed
And at dawn got up for breakfast, too much like camping,
Then went to the shed and set-to at his work.
Whenever he stopped, the hush of the trees entered him.
He listened, started again, leaned to the wood as the saw bit through
    his pencil line.
A man can be absorbed by a place until he lives its life, wears its face,
Looks out the door warily, with its eyes.
That last night he lay on the black bed and knew this,
Got up next day and walked down the track past the one workable
    farm,
Over the stepping stones of the stream,
Up the path that cuts across a spur of the hill,
Then along the grass lane until he came to Salem, where
As the tarmac passed hurriedly under the shadow of his feet
He took himself again to be the person that he was.

from *The City*

AFTERWARDS

Most people arrive
to gather on the shore
with packages
and children. The fighter

that nosed in
like the air's curious
fish, bled itself thin
over the hills.

"Here we are."
The bald statement
like the man, who shoulders
a suitcase and takes

a son by the arm. They
disappear over Earth's
trails. Did you ever
see things so strange.

STONY

Don't be surprised
by the lapidary
style of their lives.
They weren't great readers.

It's a puzzle
what they believed, and whether
they felt a surge
transforming to fear.

Calm night after rain
the houses glistened
and dripped. They were safe.
I thought I heard

explosions, but it was
only the town's fireworks,
celebrating
the will to go on.

CATASTROPHE

The family in black
like an embroidery. I can see
the mother, the serious
father, and the child.

Nobody holds
its hand. The faces are white
and European.
I know where they

collected such angst.
Centuries grip
them at the collar.
Even if they've left

the land, and the man
manages a stern
degree of fortitude,
the backs of the eyes

flash fear. Elusive
as creatures startled at
night, I think
they're beautiful.

CLEARING FORESTS

from the coast
until the mountains
slow them down. My
friends! Bad habits
like a clap on the shoulder –
"He's a good un" –
Shaking trees from their sockets
like weeds
piled into flames.
Neighbourly, they move on.

AT A PARTY

"The man who broods is lost,"
he sipped his drink.
"I'd almost like to say it isn't true."
Nodding a deprecating smile,
he turned and steered through knots of guests
holding his glass by its stem
at shoulder height.
In the sombre barque of his expensive suit
he had the grace of a fat man
who dances well.

YES

Every day, now,
an experiment,
giving new meaning
to the word culture.
Wherever I look
bacilli
multiply in rods
no faith can explain.
It's a hard shining.

SURVIVAL

I can't party any more –
that squaring of the shoulders.
What are the gaps between
physics and me? The soul's
melted away like Wordsworth's
cloud. On all the ridges of these hills
I've walked with the ants
on the blade of a bone.

BIG STORM

Tell them about me
when the masks
are down. "Can I
get through." Yes.
Water seethes
over the breakwater.
"Shall I hold." Yes
hold. "Shall I
hold." Yes, hold.

ANGLE

Each room has a mirror,
for a small town likes to see
itself as art, Dutch interiors
the outposts of their spare
design. I've seen too many
betrayals from the walls
and had enough of eyes
reversed, demanding something
with a glancing blow,
that nothing ever said
made me prepared to give.

SMALL TOWN

The umbilical accord
is broken. "What have I done
to deserve you being here.
They're so good to me,
my boys." Better than daughters?
"Yes. Yes. Oh everybody knows me
in the streets. Reputation,
the chink of solid coin
thrown down." Wheel her out,
a queen among servants.

MOTHER

"Help!
Do you think I'm
a bucket or
a shelf? I'm
down with the stone
worms. In a few
years your memories
will coalesce.
The camera
lucida will
reconstruct me. I'll
be, ghostly as
a window for souls."

REALITY

I wear my face now
like a shield though
I cannot prevent
the heat loss from my

eyes. "Where were you
when you needed
me most?" Mother sit
back and let us

admire the grace
you have acquired.
Twisted and old like
seawood in the sand.

.

END

She didn't want to die,
but a great force
pushed her out beyond the mask.
"Oh it's like breathing air
from a cold blue sky."
Her face was impassive
in the morgue.

FLOWERS

Keep on,
they say from their wounds,
how can you turn back,
we press you to the edge
with softness
that embodies no more than our lives
leaning into the future.

INHUMAN

I walk on the hill's green
wave and look down the vertiginous
slope to the trough where a house
is flotsam that would rise
on a wind- and light-whipped
peak, if there were time. Kings
of the moment are about me:
a lapwing following its cries
over the moor, and a wheatear
flicking cream-and-buff on a grey
stone, as if it were light
come alive, no time for a shadow.

from *Heroes*

HEROES

We were the first ones to ride a car to the top of the mountain,
bump-driving it higher and higher over tussocky heather and whin.
    – Come on Reg, come on!
And Bill half-running, half-stooping before us, straining to lift and
    tumble aside lichened boulders.
Bump – bump – bump – bump –. Come on Reg, come on!
And we jumped up and down on the running boards
                    – Come on, come on!
and we made it, God's marvels, because we were young.

Subdued suddenly by the massed lines of hills on all sides
      that had once been a plateau
and the river as it glistened and twisted in the deep valley
      to the sea.

Heyoooh, heyoooohh – we shouted thinly –
heyoooooh, in the great mass of the air.

THE ONE LAPWING

The one lapwing wheeling away from me
                                    wailing
as I passed a junked car high on the hill side
up to the axles in heather

like an abandoned thought

CATS

Let us be a rug
for your heart, killers
of note in the world of voles,
and sparrows. Let our

paws be soft as kiddies'
toys, and our eyes
eastern doors with a cold
curtain. Let our

excesses count for
nothing in the scale, like
fishy breath. We
preen under the rattle

of mistle thrush warnings.
Here we are
with the claw's camaraderie
at one with your selves.

THE BEACH

Walking along the beach
the crunch of shells under foot
the crisp snow of a deep summer's
deep winter, and small crabs
belly up, the sea's pets waiting
to be tickled by life,

and jelly fish too high
never to refloat, slip off,
the pulsing night-water's bells.

NOTES FROM THE CARBONIFEROUS

Night. Lightning flickers without sound.
A breeze shivers through a forest of ferns.
Dawn. Blue sky washed clean. Fronds
shutter out light. Green shade. Insect hum.
Night. Clouds massed at dusk burst.
Ferns bend low, lower, under the weight of rain.
Dawn again. Two scorpions dart-stabbing
ride each other to death. Insect hum.
Night. Not a sound, stillness a being
That's come up close, there in the dark.
Dawn again. A lizard basks, utter attention
and inattention, head a bronze rock. Night.
The tick and tap of water after rain.

RED SPIDERS

Red spiders, just hatched,
running across sun-warmth of a wall
over lichen like bits of red lichen

in all directions at once
as if they'd spilled from a scalding pot
and couldn't stop till they cooled.

A microscope would zoom up
their humourless eyes, the mouth,
eight legs' relentless traction over the pitted

terror-surface of the stone,
while the eye bent over the lens
reflects on the relevance of scale.

BARNACLES

Barnacles clamped so hard to the rock they become crusty
                                        outgrowths,
fluted visionaries by the sea's roar, the land's gates.
What is it that they wish to kiss.
As if life had become inoperable and they'd drilled
                                themselves to stone.
Move on. The next storm rises to magnificence
over the horizon.

THE LOST WOODS

The lost woods where a fox
turned startled to see us
and cast itself out of Eden.

We measured the trees'
cubic worth of cream wood
as our children picked arms-

full of bluebells. Look!
Their faces shine in the stories
still. No, we can't look,

glancing instead at the computer
where columns of figures
jerk up onto the screen.

DAWN CHORUS

Birds try out
notes like torches in
a cave, too weak
to penetrate to

walls or roof. First one
then more, tangling beams
of songs like tiny
searchlights, night
being the first chamber of

death. The survivors
sing on, each song's torch
wired to the dynamo
of blood and bone.

2 A.M.

The barn owls shriek across the night
as if there were nothing there, no branch where they perch,
no stream fumbling its way across the valley floor.

Their cries try to measure if there's such a thing as distance
and whether they should launch from wherever they are
on whatever it is that flaps and makes them feel buoyant
      and may one day be called wings.

A SHOAL OF FISH

A shoal of fish
shimmers its cloth then bursts
to a star-flower

re-forms, swerves, darts, veers
an electric alertness
stinging stragglers back

into the cloud of animate
leaves. To die
is to be alone.

SHARKS

Going nowhere but
knowing where they're
going; carrying with them
cartilagenous
needs; eyes that can't
blink in murkiest
waters; appearing out
of nothing behind
them; following mouths into
nothing before them.

THE SHRIKE

On a day grey as the shrike in its tree
when it seemed it and I were the only living things in the
    clearing
where smashed debris of undergrowth and marsh grass
    were stiff with frost,
I stopped to watch the bird twist and duck its head
then dip quickly to a ditch
rising like the winter's phoenix to a branch
with a wriggling object in its beak.
The shrike looked here and there in no hurry
and the thing wriggled its legs against the sky
a puppet in a play
where death was a function of the scene.

GHOSTS

I

A blank in life
stamped censored. The page
fresh as the scent of cut
grass. Hurry on
to the black-and-white print
of the acceptable. You know

what's hurting
and can never be amended.

"I must do it, I must"
Behind the locked door
like a confession
preceding an event. "I
must" Or a mantra
to be said and said, until

she was released
from the restraining mind
and opening her veins
could see the soul
a thin red bird.

Banging his hands against the wall
as if he had crawled to this place

When they faced each other, a silence
not to be breached by anything

there was to say (And an insect
that night with veins in its wings

like a net of fire, the thorax
flexing as it clung to the glass,

a splash of anger)

He remembered her hands,
hands that could suddenly speak –
Please, please

He was aghast
There was nothing he could do
but fling himself

into that fiery night,
rejecting her and rejecting himself
to live on the edge

with darkness above,
darkness below

"I have paced up and down.
I have made cobble stones
out of my heart. I wear
a long black winter coat
under this street lamp, in this square,
where I thought you would never
come. Please say you will remember this
when you leaf through the emptiness
you are."

"Under these covers
are you afraid. Listen
to the night, how deep

it is. It holds out silence
like a reward.

Tomorrow I'll pack
and board the plane,
letting you go, in grief.
Listen to the night
listening. Aren't you afraid."

In daytime the distance,
spreading like snow in a forest.
She butters toast, makes coffee.
The light outside is winter white

and a flock of waxwings inhabits a tree
like judgment. It's a pity,
this indifference, each moment
having to be simple and clear,

not wanting to break open like a shell.

"I reject you now. You are
nothing to me. The past is a blank,
snow drifting in footsteps
of someone who wandered there,
saw a shrike's cruelty in a bush
heard the goldcrests'
miniature animations in the firs;
waiting to be freed."

II

We'll haunt each other
ghosts in black on white

among the trees (snow
is our weather, and pain)

circle each other endlessly
crossing printless tracks
that could be yours,
be mine, leaving no trace.

"There's no end to it.
When I dip my hand
into the cold dark pool
of those days, you're

there. I withdraw the hand
and look at it. It's
followed me so many years
patient as a dog."

Ice and snow, their
crunch in the forest,
and the great black woodpecker
flapping round and round,

slapping itself onto
trees with its screams
like the soul in fear.
I left myself there.

"I'd made a house
out of my life for you
to come back to. No one
can stand the forest's

bleakness for long.
I'd arranged the cushions
in the chairs.
And you never came."

It was winter, winter.
I went to the lakes
to see ice thicken,
the mute swan

trapped in a slush hole,
thrash and fail,
the head rising and curling,
dying on its stalk.

"The past is too black
to remember. To forget.
We'll circle each other
until we die.

Remember how I waited
for you in the square
in a long black winter coat,
anxious till you came."

MOTHER

"Stop my heart
from crashing like a lost
bird into the
glass, there to see
itself in the instant
before death; found
after with a bubble
of blood at its beak."

SELF PORTRAIT BY ROTHKO

Here the face hollow and charred eyed
standing back a little in the paint,
blurred emerging and retreat
through the canvas grille.

"Life is much less than a dream,
that's why I need you.
Remember this pigment,
ambiguous proof that I did exist."

THE SEA

Off the city waves glitter with surgical needles
and thin glass vials,
white rubber gloves for handling the living
that rise and fall, the gloves
turning like magicians' hands elegantly
to show they were hiding nothing,
at dusk touching sometimes like lovers
as they move away with the tide.

HAWTHORN WAY

This is difficult terrain but we'll build on it
and before the fresh green hawthorn is weighted with rain

we'll have bulldozed through
raised walls, roofs, garages
for strangers to gaze from double-glazed windows.
Hawthorn Way where they'll be a while
neither content nor having difficult thoughts.
And we'll set up tripods over the fields for a further advance.

"Left of the hawthorn. Left,"
under the choking white scent
of its heavy-with-rain burdened boughs.

CLOUDS DRIFT

Clouds drift over a building's grey glass,

an imperturbable mirror angled against the sky

where we hoped to glimpse something other than ourselves

MY FATHER'S HANDS

My father's hands on his death bed
became like straw in the flames,
rising and swirling in the updraft
of his agony. We were afraid
to hold them, not knowing what it was
that gave them this life; afraid
we'd crush them, so they'd flail back
listless at his sides. His neck muscles
strained, his head was a hawk or a saint's.
And we had to reach out. – There. There,
gently, like handling exhausted wild birds
that still had a life-surge. – And hold them,
chained to his fluttering fingers,
weak and strong like a bird's
wings pattering inside a closed palm.

IN A RESTAURANT

The man eating alone swallows his thoughts
but cannot prevent his eyes searching the faces of the dining crowd.

When his glance is met he flicks it away, skating across the walls

as if acknowledging
the flaw in his argument.

ANGEL FISH

Angel fish were leaves of flesh
until they turned head on
in a minimal argument.

And she dressed in velvet black
shuffling up to tap the tank
lightly with a finger nail.

"It's as if they have a message
but they focus nothing
like eyes of the dead."

IT WAS ONLY POLICE

It was only police
come to find her three days dead
but whoever crawled through that hole in the door
entered a tomb
no less than a Trojan queen's
with a face mask of gold,
or a ritual tomb for the bones of a wren.

COME ON, GEORGE

That was his trick
to dance along the bar-top among bottles and drinks
in the blurred-blue smoke of our cigarettes
with his trilby at an angle
and trouser-legs flapping – Come on, George! –
and never touch a whiskey glass or a pint of beer
– Ha ha ha! – and our faces looking up at him
a hand reaching out of a sleeve
to flick ash at a tray
– Come on! Come on, George! – so he'd dance back
the long brown length of the bar, feet tapping their image
in its polish – Ha ha! Ha hah! –
hop off and take his glass,
become one of us once more.

HOW MANY GREAT SONGS

How many great songs
went out under the depthless
lid of stars without even
an echo, the folks getting up
stiff from chairs from good
listening, still clasping a
smile and what we'd call
warmth. He cut good tonight.
Yes he did. How many great
songs, while the singer
puts away his guitar, brushes
a thumb across the strings,
frets glittering in
moonlight as the mind
crisps in its frosts.

from *At the Salt Hotel*

A HILL CHAPEL

I am Death; Fear me and honour the Lord,
merciful Redeemer, say the words scrolled out of the
skeleton's mouth; but on a summer's afternoon in the hush
with sparrows cheeping in hedgerow bushes, they're

easy to dismiss; sunlight and cloud-shadow chasing
up the slopes, and a kestrel feather-dusting the sky
with its wings; only the creaking of the floorboards
as you walk about, breathing air with a dustiness

of three hundred years ago, leaves a doubt; Death
eats with Mortality, and look what a meal they've
had, the remains scattered in the graveyard;
Death getting up and saying Amen, when the pewter plates are

empty; the farmers knowing it would come to this
when they bent on large knees, if not to pray, to acquire
protective covering; the silence here is waiting, in a
way not found on the hills, for a sentence to be

finished, that might set things right; but whoever it
was has gone out into the sunlight and vanished;
what does Death think in the long interludes when
nobody comes and his words are unread; he is painted there

on the wall, a thing unholy, yet the most powerfully
present; and notice that he smiles, and has a tilt
to the head, as if deaf or partially blind, straining to
hear the curlew's cries; see the kestrel swoop to the kill.

ABOUT THE USK

If this were America, the river grumbles, I'd
be called Red and they'd make up a song
about me; I'm sure there are songs about the Usk
I say, poems too; fatuous begat fanciful, yes
the river says, I know; I mean real songs, *Which*

way, which way, does the Red River run,
that sort of thing; it turned its red back on me, a roil
of iron-blooded water; travelled fast by the
Blorenge out toward Newport and the sea; I'll
sing for you, I said; thanks, the river sneered,

I'll engage you for my hundred thousandth birthday
party; what's it like, it asked, not to be always
travelling on; what is sleep; I stir myself round in
pools from time to time, but the boredom is a cross
I throw off for the trout, those fat lozenges; I

don't know, I said, we're so different, how
to explain; I knew you when you were young, the
river says, didn't I; the one with the jam jar and
sticklebacks; a kingfisher watcher; and do you remember that
dipper walking under water right before you;

and the pair of sandpipers' light brown backs flying
away from you but never from me, the river; yes,
I said, I can never forget; you people come and
go, looking into me, trying to discover me;
you always miss the trout jump, turning for the

splash; almost seeing, almost getting it right;
you must be tired of missing out, is that why you
invented second sight; ignoring this, I turned for home;
it's a kind of song, the river shouted, taking the big
bend at Llanvihangel; remember in future to call me Red.

NANT-Y-MOCH

They said they would build the most beautiful dam ever,
the concrete skirts of a machine-age goddess
holding the water back; a tough one

who doesn't mind getting her feet wet,
or the cold; grinning at the sky; not irritated by tourists
who lean across to look along the sweeping
flow of the concrete to her toes; this

could be a new age for crucifixions,
Anno Dominae; the tourists getting back into their cars out of the
        weather;
the stream below a lost dog scurrying
after the trace of its mistress's scent, the silver
lead trailing behind it

and the concrete skirt too stiff for her
to bend and pick it up; the weight of water at her back
is the pressure she must resist, arms outstretched,

fine light-grey concrete arms touching the tips of each side of the
        valley,
face stretched above her throat to the sky
like a Victory for a modern empire recently collapsed
but living on here;

the tourists are too small for this
and squeezing into their cars seems homely again
as they cruise along the lakeside, past

the Forestry Commission firs' domestic appliances
for getting down to things and giving them a
scrub. It's late

as the last car crosses the causeway over the dam.

AT A PLACE NEAR US

They built the Ultimate Laser Machine
on top of Craig-y-Pistyll, never thinking
about the power of water to cleanse; the Machine
pointing its gadgets at the sky; it could

shatter the visor of a man walking on the
moon, that black plexi-glass wherein we
see ourselves more clearly than face to face,
the hi-de-ho antics of the one

standing by the flag, the space module's
tin can for eventual return; the Machine
was manned day and night, and hikers
re-routed past the deserted farmhouse and the

grove of spruce, its mat of needles so
soft it seemed like a deafness walking over
it; pointed at Mars, where someone waving on the
great Mons itself could have been

wiped out, like a visitation from the gods;
on the farms, people got used to it, the white dome
that housed the Machine, and the razor wire
and surveillance cameras; time is, and

nothing is like it used to be, was the saying in the
village; and the existence of the Machine softened
the economy, just as the tide at Traeth
Maelgwyn seeps into every runnel in the saltings

until the landscape floats in a
half mirror of water; and it was water they
forgot, its cleansing power; the run-off
from the Llyn pooling below the Craig, then

flowing on as a thin upland stream;
people would say What good did that ever
do, forgetting the wheatears on grey fence
posts, and dung beetles just rolling along, rolling

along, and buzzards and ravens up on high
crags, all of whom had an intimate
relation to the stream; I'm just mentioning this
as something they'd forgotten,

when at night the dome was opened
and the ray swung to point at the moon;
some say they could see the thin red beam
and the imaginary moon man raising a hand.

WHAT THE CATS ARE SAYING

Dogs, say cats, must be God's dippy
creation, not like our autonomous selves; too
much fuzz around the edges, too much of their brains
going out with that barking aggression;

we would have handled it differently, being
prime movers among the birds, and tentative
explorers of abandoned back gardens where we
find things arranged to suit ourselves;

in a stand-off, back the cats; street fighting's
not our way, in gangs, and we have the more subtle
vocabulary; a duet or quintet of wails would take
years to write down, we improvise so much;

yet the music is recognisably us; God
puts on His cat's head to try to talk to us,
but there are many mistakes made in the world of
gods; we show Him the back of indifference;

dogs, quite the contrary, need someone to
idealise; promise to be a friend for ever to
anyone who will master them, couple them to a
running lead so the boss can play jokes

jerking them back; blackbirds and wrens know we
never break a promise, we invite them to have fun
in the kill; also the mouse; young rabbits
never get the hang of our skill outside burrows;

God whips His creations in, the hound master,
but He never disturbs the cats who
can neither be saved nor damned; that is why
when killed, our pelts are left on the road.

IT SEEMS SO

Diseases know nothing, not even the permanent need for
expansion they fulfil; imagine being smallpox, last
survivors herded on the reservation of a petri dish's
gel, in a lock-and-key laboratory where they crowd and

divide and still nowhere to go, no eyes looking out of scarred
faces; or the plague lingering in swamps here and there,
the legend of the dark fisherman to see whose face is
death, as he punts silently among the reed beds, where

bitterns and spoonbills are quiet in his wake; it's
best not to name them, as a precaution, but ebola
can't be resisted, having the name of a polished black object
intended for a ritual where something went wrong;

are diseases beautiful? the theoretician of aesthetics
takes a long look at the screen of the scanning electron
microscope; she doesn't know; the virus docking with the flesh
like a Mars probe come to life at touchdown on the red soil,

the invaders and body snatchers, the ones who can peel the face
off a beautiful young woman, listless on the bed; perhaps
there are no aesthetics in nature, she suggests; it's
only us who can pick and choose; yes, that is an answer;

let's go back to the complete set of Phaidon books on European
art; chapels on dusty plains with faded portraits of
Paradise and the many lifetimes of God; whatever we have asked
is, in any case, unsolvable while the dark fisherman poles

the swamp's waterways, and on chapel walls Lazarus is
raised again, blinded by the light and what the fuss is
about, weaker than he thought and in need of his wife's
helping arm, while the neighbours crowd and look on.

AT THE SALT HOTEL

One day I'll go to the sal-
t hotel in Mali (or Cha-
d) where thirst's on everyone'-
s mind/recline in a sal-
t chair on the salt veran-
da/shaded from a sky so blu-
e it's the hands of pray-
er/and call for the waterbo-
y who'll skip across the y-
ard's hexagonals of salt th-
e unacknowledged actio-
nplan of the face of god/I'l-
l whistle for life/then whi-
stle for death (softly/becau-
se he's a travellin' man li-
ke me)/and the boy bring-
s shrimp from the salt-shru-
nk lakes/veréé goot/you tr-
y/scooping up the grey wa-
ter crawlers salt resistor-
s oxygen exchangers/mmm-
m/with a zest for the blu-
e extremes/you buy/at the sal-
t hotel/thrusting drippi-
ng and wriggling god's ner-
ves for me to see in the pail.

DEPRESSION OVERLOOKING THE BAY

Nobody talks to the fat man n-
ow/he's on a cliff/he's disconsola-
te/might as well count the fluf-
f in his pockets/ooo fat man it'-
s a long way down to the rock tha-
t looks to be floating in the quea-
sy sea where a seal stares u-
p with labrador eyes the retrie-
ving water-dog whose supper is fi-
sh/hmmm whiskers and a salty bla-
ck snout that's probably sniffi-
ng for molecules of you up ther-
e/tick off the divergence fat man oh-
h millions of years between you and th-
e seal/the sea-dog at home in a lar-
der of fat/the whale-man wonderin-
g if it's time to jump/I wouldn'-
t would you/no?/then let's shou-
t/FAT MAN COME BACK WE LOVE YOU/does-
n't matter if it's not quite true/th-
ere's no future in the rock's har-
d pillow the sea's cold sheets/FA-
T MAN YOU CAN'T DREAM THERE tel-
l him with his brains bashed and th-
e sea dipping a tongue into a worl-
d famous delicacy/ and you have to be hu-
man to know/MAKE THE CHOICE FAT MA-
N MAKE THE CHOICE/can't tell it to the fa-
mous retrieving seal whose sea is a m-
oor brimming with herrings/with the won-
derfully-barred marauder-faced mack-
erel/and it's worked/he's groping a wa-
y along the ledge dainty as a ballet dan-
cer on points/well done everyone/h-
ere he comes dislodging wi-
th his hands fragments of shale tha-
t tinkle as they trickle and boun-
ce up over the ledge past his fee-

t/ooo fat man that could be y-
ou (frightened now because h-
e sees in the giddy fall of inan-
imate stone a whole book of conse-
quences)/so well done everybod-
y well done/here he comes the wha-
le-man's return/extend him a hand.

SOUTHERN EXPOSURE

Let's sashay up the street to th-
e Dew Drop Inn/it's a summer nigh-
t and the trees are full of cicadas-
s/millions of a small crisp insec-
t's chain-saw screechings rising throu-
gh metal and nerves/the band wil-
l be there playing Old Timey (th-
ey're taking requests)/and the waitre-
ss comes quickly through the crow-
d/tray raised and balanced on the fla-
t of a hand above her shoulder/a pi-
tcher of beer and six glasses/sli-
ding between the men in pushed-ba-
ck chairs making a point/so we ca-
n see her waist is slim her face ha-
lo'd by back-lit hair/leaning int-
o our silence with the glasses (o-
ne for you/one for you)/she doesn'-
t seem to mind that our silence i-
s for her/gliding away with the empt-
y tray held high watched by the bar-
man polishing a glass/outside (I'l-
l bet) the cicadas are vibrating th-
emselves to ecstasy/little bark-gri-
ppers with bug-head mad-lamp eyes scree-
ching the just-is-ness which is natur-
e's original version of holy/und-
er a moon that's great and sickly grea-
t and inhuman without a contingen-
cy plan/the ill man's weary confess-
ion of nothing/and suddenly I'-
m lonely/and someone shouts loud t-
o the band play In the Pines.

NEW MAN

He went into detox/and what they d-
id there/came out a new man/diff-
erent human being/wouldn't say mu-
ch/the modesty in him come up har-
d against something/without words/an-
d blank as all the days he didn't thin-
k would be there to come/the magn-
ox clean they say/thanks to him an-
d his team/where are they/stand up stan-
d up/at parades and special days/the man wh-
o made it safe/who made it/never to tel-
l/sitting up straight at dusk/proppe-
d by a blue silk cushion/blue as caesiu-
m in dreams/watching the screen/watchi-
ng the stream of blue particles o-
f light/this is what it is/being safe.

AT ABERAERON

That was a day/the tide swelli-
ng through the bottleneck har-
bour entrance in long rapid ro-
lls/long striding shocks/and th-
e fat man beside me troubled/(wi-
ll a matchbox hold his soul)/a-
nd two yachts riding the inshore s-
ea one north one south masts pre-
ssed flat by the buffeting win-
d until the sails nearly drag-
ged in cold flashes of foam/me-
n rigged with safety-lines far ou-
t over the side helping the dee-
p fin of the keel stave off a foun-
dering yaw/I'd like to have yelle-
d and let the wind tear up my voi-
ce/for the zest of it/as the ya-
chts passed dipping and lurchi-
ng/masts nearly touching/death and li-
fe at the helm arguing who was bes-
t/and the men with no time stret-
ched over the flouncing shearing wa-
ter gripping a grim trapeze/sh-
uddering past north and south into th-
e roil of sky and sea rock and cliff/l-
eaving me at the harbour wall wi-
th the fat man wrapped in a coa-
t of silence with his hands glov-
ed in silence/backs to the town and i-
ts interior concerns/two human-
s with scanning eyes and brains too bi-
g to be content/admiring the commo-
tion of those bone-shaken rider-
s oilskins streaming over bra-
ced flesh no time to wipe spra-
y from the eyes taste the salt sma-
ck of life on the lips/come o-
n said the fat man let's go home.

SEE YOU THERE

I'm thinking of the place where they sai-
d they found water/not on the map/no-
t trudged to for a long day over the m-
oor/not the pool's shallow dish for the seraphi-
m to sip from when nobody's there/fo-
r the freshwater biologist to net the scraw-
l of water crawlers and sediment wrigg-
lers/I'm thinking of the place where they sai-
d they found water/more like the place f-
or the tired horses set two miles out of tow-
n where the water trickles from a car-
ved mouth into the stone trough/pea-
ce and resistance to the persecu-
tors trotting by with the whips of bankers'
drafts/and peace to the administrators car-
ving the minutes on the back of a wo-
man/the place they said took endur-
ance then freedom from desire for deliver-
ance/I've said enough/it's un-
der the great drift of stars we forme-
d from/the snowdrift of light/it'-
s there in the eyes of the owl and the bru-
sh of the woman who painted the ow-
l who will be forgotten/I'm not taking my coa-
t or any sandwiches/if I get th-
ere (or don't) it will be sufficient.

TWO SKULLS

What was the taste of diges-
tive biscuits/what was the ta-
ste of taste's expectan-
cy the nose and its membra-
ne over a plate of steaming bea-
ns salted and buttered/wha-
t was the integument of finger-
s doing touching that other's ski-
n/what was the phallus's ru-
bber intelligence its ga-
ngleader acts/what were the ey-
es doing looking into h-
er eyes and her eyes loo-
king into his/what tricked u-
s into disarticu/what was br-
eath the comfort of lu-
ngs the ribs' slow rising and fa-
lling/what was the throat a-
nd kissing her throat/wh-
at tricked us here/trapp-
ed us and grew us and thr-
ew us down/what brutality at the bo-
ne-mounds showed us the way.

OVER TO YOU

Cars put a brave face on i-
t/they need biology to kee-
p them going/in magnificent sho-
wrooms where paintwork's a whi-
sper of gloss a touch of a glo-
ve/where chrome's the mirro-
r to be held at all conceivabl-
e angles to the sun/upholster-
y waits for the pat of a hand pe-
dals the soft depression of a foo-
t/in plate-glass cars are a drea-
m of their own charm/the showr-
oom manager has the steps of a poodl-
e/there's brilliance in the ai-
r a cathedral's sanctity release-
d like helium under strip-ligh-
ts palms in corner pots aloof wi-
th the elegance of fashionable mer-
chant banks/and price-tags per-
ched on roofs like the world's rar-
est birds come to the hand/ye-
t needing biomachines to perfor-
m/the acceptable cheque and ingra-
tiating smile/for the steel-bl-
ue mercedes to murmur out of the d-
oor/a hint of exhaust the brea-
th of leather and steel/dri-
ver at the wheel whoever you ar-
e... pray the machines/then it'-
s out onto ordinary streets/th-
e bonnet pointing to destin-
y that is always ahead wherev-
er it goes/a biomachine strapp-
ed in and obedient/looking pa-
st the wipers on a rainy day bu-
t not at humans at the crossing/h-
eads down/who are not the sum of any-
thing in the hymnal of machines.

THE LOGIC IN IT

Reverse engineer the molecul-
ar spring of the proboscis of a bu-
tterfly and see how it uncoil-
s in the delights of a flowe-
r/so much to be done we allow nan-
osmiles only at the bar after han-
ging up our coats/it was a col-
d day at the laboratory col-
d for June like the blue puls-
e of a thought across a brain scann-
ed on the monitor/only machine-
s only macheeenes sang the assis-
tant washing petri dishes at th-
e sink watching the campus girl-
s pass by/biopsy being the rewar-
d for having got this far x-r-
ays being the pay-off for seei-
ng things out/though not for th-
e butterflies on the Tennessee bri-
dge the monarchs' wings floppi-
ng with the breeze on the grou-
nd like keeled over loveli-
ness in strident autumn ligh-
t/as for the future Huxley T-
ee Aitch always knew there would b-
e no woman's breast to soothe his tem-
ples saying how is my dar-
ling how is my darling now.

PREPARATIONS FOR THE FINAL ASSAULT

The role is a small one and easy to get
wrong; then he is shot, running down a bombed out
street where the last unidentified sniper gets his

man, or shot in the head at a summary court martial,
his life the shrug of an officer's shoulders,
another bullet loaded in the breech; the message

gets through to mother and father; "He was an ordinary
boy"; the tanks and apv's are fuelled, blue smoke
chokes the air, icy mud creams as the tracks

execute a right-hand slide toward the city, and jets
fly in low with messages for widows; the night
was silent except for the barking of a dog, and snow

held off, only a few flakes came winnowing down
among the stiff withies, brushing lightly off the fabric
of the tents; at home they're holding a vigil; one

hundred thousand candles in the square, glittering
like the lights in eyes; and a priest is denouncing this
war, calling on Jesus; but there is no having done with it

yet; so the jets fly back to the burning city, with jokes
written on the bombs; why did they start a winter
war? because mud covers the acts of the victors; meanwhile

defenders dig in on wooded slopes, not looking up
at the sound of the shells' beautiful parabolas; to be alive
and in a place like this, the heart shut down and cold.

HIS FIRST PUBLIC STATEMENT

Allow me to introduce myself, Virtual
Man; I killed in Texas once, but who
and what for are not asked; I am the
syndication of the human heart; did they think about

that when they wheeled me from the execution
chamber; the lab assistants whistling as they
sliced me into virtuality from my scalp
to my toes; here is the brain, here the pancreas;

the girl student clicks on the part
she wants; I am unreal, yet she knows me
better than a lover; at lunch she
goes out with bare arms to meet friends,

and nerves are left on screen in a fine
veneer; the sections could not be thinner
but they found no trace of a soul;
she thinks I'm pixels and light,

not someone unaccommodated once
who would have watched her walk down the
street; that pavement ease of the young in
summer men hunger for; thank you

for listening, it has helped; and now she's
back, scrolling down with a mouse
under the ball of her palm; remember
I am only here to be understood.

IN THE DAYS WHEN HE WAS STRONG

What war were you in Bri? The Alcohol
War, nineteen-fifty-six to ninety-nine; left
leg lost to cider in a slow attrition of country
pubs where I parked the van in leafy shade,

where yellowhammers seeped and sizzled in the
hedgerow; right went to whisky; I'll save the knee,
the Doctor said; but I said Don't bother,
I've finished walking in the shadows of the town; the eye

came out like a rotten plum; that was
the rearguard; rum beating its drum; if I can
get someone to roll me out of the Home,
I can still spend a night at the bar; whisky

and beer there too, veterans all, hostility
forgotten; just a pint, just a pint; that won't
put out my light for ever; mulling over the death toll,
tall tales, and a life well spent.

THE DRIVE SOUTH

Newsagents' lights shining off wet pavements,
the night's glue coming unstuck in all the villages
from Caernarfon to Dolgellau, traffic lights no longer
playing the staring game in empty streets;

but what was that on the long haul earlier,
packing cardboard, or a camel hair coat, or
a beast swerved around in the driving on; the road

is usually littered with mysteries, unsolved; the
broken glance in a pedestrian's eyes; for the drive's
duration it's best to off-load the mind like emptying
pockets at the police station, where it's someone else's

job to docket the contents in a numbered bag.

A CITRUS GROVE

These wasps drunk as Chinese po-
ets crawling stumblingly over a grapefrui-
t's ruin/where it fell from a bu-
sh among lemons and oranges that fe-
ll too to rot in the green alley li-
ke a planetary disaster/the grapefrui-
t scaled with a curd of moul-
d fermenting the brew for these insec-
t swiggers/as I was saying/these was-
ps/legs buckling on a drunken spr-
ee have somewhere built a paper nes-
t so delicate a woman I knew once as-
ked is it art?/no it isn't/it's ar-
t/no/it's art/no/no/wrong eve-
n though she had one perched on a si-
deboard so it looked contrived/(con-
text isn't everything)/these was-
ps/self-propelling stingers that nobo-
dy likes are fine by me/and I'-
d have one of their nests by me t-
oo/an absorption lantern gathering li-
ght/to remind me nature's never sai-
d a thing about itself/except us (ar-
e we nature?)/the whorls and wra-
p-around papier mâché grey as untr-
eated wood in a down-town slum.

ON THE USK

Let's praise the dipper/mountain strea-
m balancer on chill stones/voice los-
t in the background clatter of water/un-
der-water walker performing the last of the Fou-
r Impossible Tasks/gambler on loneli-
ness on the high moor where fir-
s quilt the land in folds/not notice-
d in the fine thin upland summer by ram-
blers passing over crushed sedge in a li-
ne of woollen socks and boots par-
kas and maps taking in the wide swee-
p and forgetting the detail/bes-
t seen in rapid shallows where the broken-u-
p light makes it a dark runner/th-
ere/and then/there/the white-bibbed bo-
bber on stones looking out over the wa-
ter-world the alliance of light and we-
t and hardness and air that's its now a-
nd when we've gone taking down the bir-
d book in the living room or looki-
ng closely at the miniature on the wal-
l and saying yes looking again a-
nd wondering how the artist brushe-
d in paint the nerves and the brightne-
ss the tremulous liquid glance of th-
e little plump stream-creeper's eye.

NIGHT SCENE

Look at the moths hov-
ering at spikes of flower-
s/the space docks of a bu-
sh/hunger hardwired to wi-
ngs/inflight harmonics a-
bove hearing/wingbeats a bei-
ge snow/watch on/the nigh-
t isn't done/a bat whi-
zzes its eccentric arc-
s around the house the bla-
ck traps of trees /Hallo! Hal-
lo! its echo locatio-
n banging it away from wa-
lls but ruffling back fr-
om the furry flakes of mo-
ths/night morsels sla-
mmed into the stomach sa-
c/is it a shame thi-
s is the way life gets along.

CONVERSATION ON THE RHOLBEN

Ancestors to the hawks?/be-
tter look for theropods tucked u-
p in strata great experimenters w-
ith fearlessness and reckless jum-
ping/proto-feathered risk frea-
ks with warm blood and cool brai-
ns/some the size of chickens to b-
e sported on the wrist of go-
d the palaeo-falconer's pri-
de/removing the hood of pity fr-
om their eyes/letting them scoo-
t along steamy animal trails t-
o see what they can find/bursti-
ng out to grip-trap lizzards l-
eap and snatch down dragonflie-
s in a tangle of cerise and ce-
llophane struts/dinosaur brain-
s packed above the inability to sc-
ream/and here (now) the kestr-
el trembling its wings over a sl-
ope of bracken/and a beetle rolli-
ng dung the monstrousness of th-
e task like the fabulous mechan-
ical talking dummy/helloimnigelh-
owdoyoudo/helloimnigelhowdoyoud-
o helloimnige-l/only disengaged b-
y the bird as it swoops to clut-
ch and crack its casing and th-
e whirring and whizzing sto-
p/the bird crouched under frett-
ed bracken with an appetite for ar-
thropods swallowing black exoske-
leton in a green silence und-
er clouds that fleece the af-
ternoon sky/(and hasn't it been a lov-
ely day with all this space an-
d loneliness/but time to be gett-
ing back to the car tomorrow be-
ing Monday and an early start).

A TOAST

Have you seen those wor-
ms that dehydrate in Antarc-
tica to be blown almo-
st weightless by a deser-
t wind/until in a spo-
t with a touch of moistur-
e/a degree less cold/th-
ey rehydrate and carry o-
n in the regolith/that'-
s adaptation/ada/p/tatio-
n/where my brain and y-
ours would expand with i-
ce (have to) and the eye-
s two crystal balls on ho-
ld/so here's to the nema-
todes/desert-disaster-wi-
nd-blast-survivors/t-
ectonic travellers livi-
ng because they have to be-
cause they have to five mi-
llion years in the cold.

CRINOIDS

A stack of dollars spilled o-
n the Permian baize/and there're
e more (look closely)/columns of ann-
ular stalks toppled in mud whe-
n the deal went down and chair-
s were thrown back from time'-
s gamble with life/it was a dar-
k night it was many dark nigh-
ts when the sea lilies wil-
ted in seas become too cold t-
oo deep/were mown down in the wa-
ter fields their bad luck scatt-
ered among the cards that led to u-
s/and me here sizing a red chun-
k of stone in the hand percei-
ving how they fell in waving sw-
athes and decayed/piles of stal-
k-discs rolled loose by water ac-
tion becoming an idea of themsel-
ves in stone/being (too) like u-
s (and the whole seething saloo-
n) gamblers whose coins were thems-
elves who didn't give a damn.

PALAEOZOIC

Cyanobacteria crowd the pool-
s/blue-green blooms the near-
est life's come yet to prett-
y flowers/winter rains are pa-
st and heat on the plains lif-
ts off the water's delicate ski-
n layer after layer/till the al-
gae are herded in a tepid ma-
ss/till reduced to stain-
s in mud that's baked and cra-
cked like palm-skin on psy-
chotics' hands/whose bodies li-
sten to the mind saying li-
fe has no water/that right n-
ow and forever there's nowher-
e to go/could be the mad bl-
okes are right/look aroun-
d/all Earth listening to the sk-
y's one-off conversation-
al monotone/shuffling to th-
e algorithm blues/baloo-ba-
lues/oh those baloo-green ba-
lues/syncopate it up a litt-
le now/c'mon ever'body si-
ng along/baloo-baloo balue-gr-
een blues/yeah!/mmm-hmmm/ba-
loo-baloo balue-green blues.

Acknowledgements

The poems selected here are taken from: *Borderland* (Mariscat, 1984); *Lightning Country* (Dangaroo, 1987); *Clay* (Headland, 1989); *The Confirmation* (Gomer, 1992); *The City* (Gomer, 1993); *Heroes* (Gomer, 1996); and *At the Salt Hotel* (Headland, 2003).

Author's note: This is a selection of poems published between 1984 and 2003, excluding the narrative poem *Ice* (Gomer, 2001). Some of the poems from *Heroes*, originally untitled, have been given titles for this edition, while minor revisions have been incorporated into a few poems throughout. The chapbook *Clay* is included in its entirety.

My thanks to Helle Michelsen and Pamela Stewart for their helpful criticism over the years. Also to Amy Wack at Seren for her meticulous editing.